GOLD MEDA

Golden tips for
your first TROPICAL

AQUARIUM

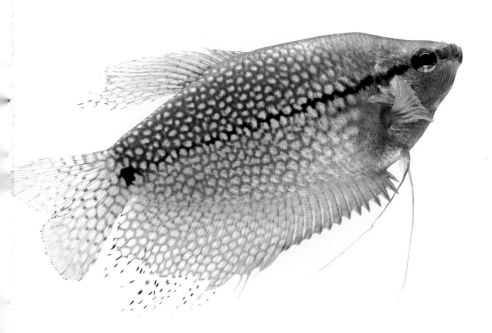

PETER HISCOCK

Interpet Publishing

The Author Peter Hiscock
began keeping fish as a child,
inspired by his parents, both
accomplished marine biologists.
He was appointed manager of a
retail aquatic outlet at just 17
years of age and went on to
complete aquatic studies at
Sparsholt College in Hampshire,
UK. He entered publishing with
contributions to the aquatic press
and has since written several
books. His interests include fish
behaviour and the natural
habitats of aquarium species.

Editorial: Ideas into Print
Designer: Phil Clucas MSIAD
Photography: Geoff Rogers
© Interpet Publishing
Production management:
Consortium, Poslingford, Suffolk
Print Production:
Sino Publishing House Ltd.
Printed and bound in China

Published by Interpet Publishing,
Vincent Lane, Dorking,
Surrey RH4 3YX, England

ISBN 10   1 84286 140 9
ISBN 13   978 1 84286 140 0

*The recommendations in this
book are given without any
guarantees on the part of the
author and publisher. If in doubt,
seek the advice of a veterinarian
or tropical fish specialist.*

Contents

INTRODUCTION

Why do tropical fish make popular pets?

Fish cannot be held, stroked, played with or walked, so what makes them one of the most popular pets throughout the world? One answer is that we enjoy watching these beautiful animals and how they behave, and caring for a self-contained world that relies completely upon us, the fishkeepers. We can learn from tropical fish; to keep them successfully we must understand something about biology and chemistry, which helps us to appreciate the natural world. Fish are interesting creatures as well; with hundreds to choose from, each one has its own character and distinct style of behaviour. These qualities, combined with a relative ease of keeping and low running costs, makes tropical fish the ideal pets for people from all walks of life.

Right: This beautiful cichlid, the ram (Mikrogeophagus ramirezi) will do well, given the right conditions and care in the aquarium.

The underwater environment

The most obvious difference between fish and other pets is that fish live in water and this is what makes their care so different. Fishkeepers are often referred to as 'aquarists' because keeping fish is much more about maintaining their environment – the aquarium – than the fish themselves. If you provide the right aquarium conditions, maintain the quality of the water and feed them properly, your tropical fish will look after themselves.

Right: Setting up a successful tropical aquarium, furnished with healthy plants and stocked with a colourful fish, means learning how to provide the best underwater environment.

Female

Male

*Above: Cherry barbs are under
threat in the wild, but widely bred
in Far Eastern fish farms.*

The aquarium trade

Most tropical freshwater aquarium fish are captive-bred
on a large scale in places such as South America and
Singapore before being transported to shops. Some are
still caught from the wild, and
this is usually done with care
rather than destructively.
In the vast majority of cases,
if aquarium fishes become
rare in the wild it is due to the
destruction of their habitats,
rather than because they
are being caught for the
aquarium trade. Some
common, captive-bred
aquarium fish are actually
extinct in the wild and only
continue to exist because
of their popularity as pets.

*GOLD
MEDAL
TIPS*

***FISH ARE GOOD FOR
YOUR HEALTH***
*Studies have shown that people
who keep fish are more healthy
and have happier relationships
compared to population
averages, and the relaxing
effect of keeping fish is well
documented in many cultures.*

IDEAL PETS FOR CHILDREN
*Aquarium fish are great pets for
children. However, fish are living
animals that require the correct
care and mistakes are easy to
make, so supervise young
fishkeepers closely.*

*Above: Children are fascinated
by aquarium fish, which offer a
glimpse into the natural world.*

TAKE IT STEADY
*You cannot buy an aquarium
and set it up with fish all at once,
since keeping fish successfully
relies on providing a stable,
matured environment. Planning
is essential; be prepared to take
your time setting up your tank
and stocking it slowly over a
period of weeks and months.*

A SENSITIVE NATURE

Fish are highly sensitive to changes in their environment, including events that happen outside the aquarium. For this reason it is important to avoid sudden changes in light or movement – and you should never tap on the aquarium glass.

ADAPTATIONS

The shape of a fish's body offers clues to the kind of aquarium it needs; streamlined or 'torpedo-shaped' fish are designed for open-water swimming, while tall, compressed fish are more suited to gliding through plants. The direction of the mouth and the presence or lack of barbels indicates whether the fish is a top, middle or bottom feeder.

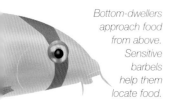

An upturned mouth indicates that the fish feeds at the water surface, approaching its food from below.

A fish with a terminal mouth can approach its food head-on, taking items from the surface and the bottom.

Bottom-dwellers approach food from above. Sensitive barbels help them locate food.

Can fish learn and remember?

No-one is sure where the 'three-second memory' myth originated but, as any aquarist will tell you, it is entirely untrue. Fish actually have quite a capacity to learn and to remember any event that helps or threatens their survival. Many fish will learn to recognise their owner (or whoever feeds them), becoming active and excited at feeding time. They will also choose preferred hiding spots and recognise their tankmates as well as become familiar with the daily aquarium routine, such as when the lights go on and off.

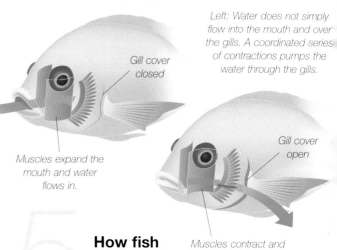

Left: Water does not simply flow into the mouth and over the gills. A coordinated series of contractions pumps the water through the gills.

Gill cover closed

Muscles expand the mouth and water flows in.

Gill cover open

Muscles contract and push water over the gills.

How fish breathe

Like us, fish need oxygen to survive and while we get our oxygen from the air, fish get theirs from water. As fish take in water through the mouth, it passes over the gills. These contain a series of blood vessels where oxygen can move from the water to the fish's blood through a thin membrane. The dissolved oxygen comes from the surrounding air and enters at the water surface. If the surface is agitated by a filter or airpump, more oxygen can enter the water. Because fish can absorb oxygen from the water, they can also absorb pollutants and toxins, which is why maintaining good water quality is such an important part of fishkeeping.

BASIC BIOLOGY

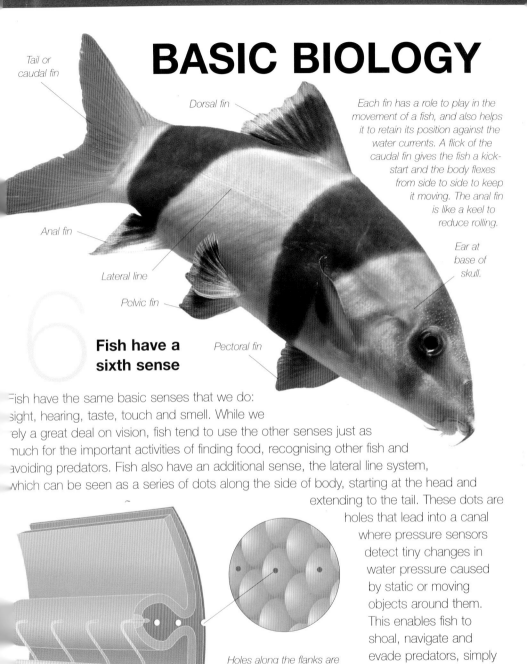

Tail or caudal fin

Dorsal fin

Each fin has a role to play in the movement of a fish, and also helps it to retain its position against the water currents. A flick of the caudal fin gives the fish a kick-start and the body flexes from side to side to keep it moving. The anal fin is like a keel to reduce rolling.

Anal fin

Ear at base of skull.

Lateral line

Pelvic fin

Fish have a sixth sense

Pectoral fin

Fish have the same basic senses that we do: sight, hearing, taste, touch and smell. While we rely a great deal on vision, fish tend to use the other senses just as much for the important activities of finding food, recognising other fish and avoiding predators. Fish also have an additional sense, the lateral line system, which can be seen as a series of dots along the side of body, starting at the head and extending to the tail. These dots are holes that lead into a canal where pressure sensors detect tiny changes in water pressure caused by static or moving objects around them. This enables fish to shoal, navigate and evade predators, simply by sensing where objects are, how big they are and in what direction they are moving.

Holes along the flanks are openings to the lateral line, a sensory organ system that responds to pressure waves, making fish aware of nearby objects.

FISH VARIETIES

All shapes and sizes

There are literally hundreds of aquarium fish to choose from, with new species appearing regularly, and much of the difficulty associated with successful fishkeeping comes from being able to choose the right mixture of species. Good dealers will be able to offer advice on all the species they sell, but it is always a good idea to research any fish you intend to buy. Remember that most fish on sale will be young and their size and temperament can change significantly as they get older.

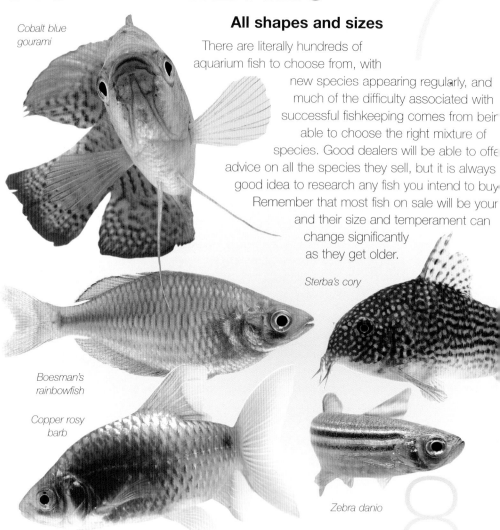

Cobalt blue gourami

Sterba's cory

Boesman's rainbowfish

Copper rosy barb

Zebra danio

Mixing fish from different groups

Most popular tropical aquarium fish can be put in groups, such as barbs, tetras, gouramis, danios, rainbowfishes, livebearers, cichlids, catfish and loaches. The fish within a group usually share similar requirements and behaviours in the aquarium, but there are always exceptions to the rule. A mixture of different types makes for an interesting and varied aquarium, with fish swimming at all levels – surface, midwater and bottom.

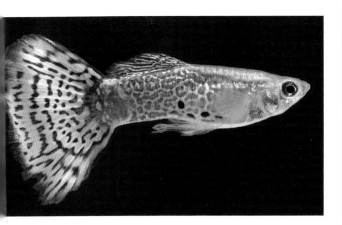

Above: The long, flowing tails of the male guppy are a great temptation to fin-nipping fish. Harassed fish become stressed and susceptible to disease.

What is meant by 'community fish'?

The term 'community fish' is often used to describe a species that lives happily with other peaceful fishes. It is a good idea to use the term as a guide only, as not all community fish will co-exist without causing problems. For example, a fish that is likely to nip at long-finned species may still be considered a community fish because it will live perfectly happily in a community of fishes without long fins. Some quieter-natured fish prefer to be kept in a peaceful environment and may become stressed if kept with overactive species, yet both may still be described as community fish.

The term 'community fish' is therefore a good starting point, but you should always check the individual needs of the fish you intend to house together.

Right: Otocinclus catfish rasp on algae, helping to keep it under control. Provide algae wafers if natural levels get low.

GOLD MEDAL TIPS

COLOUR TYPES
Some fish have been specially bred to produce different colour types or to have long fins, giving the fishkeeper a wider choice. Although most of these bred forms are ideal for aquarium life some, such as the guppy, are often less resistant to disease due to overbreeding.

A STEP TOO FAR
On occasion, practices emerge in the hobby that are harmful to fish, simply in order to increase profits. These include injecting fish with bright inks or developing deformed fish, such as 'fresh-water parrotfish'. As a whole, the industry is very responsible and only a tiny minority of shops sell such fish.

WORKER FISH
Some species of fish perform a useful role in the aquarium by disturbing the substrate and preventing the build-up of debris, or eating unsightly algae. A mixture of scavengers and algae-eaters help to keep the aquarium looking clean, but still need feeding with specialised foods.

Tiger barb

SQUABBLES ARE GOOD
Some fin-nipping fish, such as the infamous tiger barb, are much better behaved when kept in large numbers. This is because the fin-nipping habit is an extension of the fish's natural squabbling nature. If the group is large enough, the fish remain occupied with each other and ignore other fish.

BOUNDARY MARKERS
Fish use objects such as rocks and wood to define territories in an aquarium. If a fish is causing trouble because of its territorial behaviour, moving the tank decor around will remove established territories, creating a more even 'balance of power' within the tank.

LINE OF SIGHT
Many territorial fish will only act aggressively towards fish within immediate sight. Creating areas of dense, tall plants and breaking the tank into distinct areas will help fish to stay out of the sight of aggressive individuals.

10

Don't let aggression get out of control

Most fish show some level of aggression. In some cases it is a natural and healthy part of their lifestyle; in others it can result in bullying and stress, causing physical damage, disease and even the death of an unlucky victim. Groups of small fish often fight periodically, but this is simply to reinforce each fish's status within a group and rarely causes harm. In some species, such as many livebearers, males can constantly harass females in order to breed. To avoid excessive stress amongst livebearers, either keep only one sex, or keep twice as many females as males so that the aggression is spread more thinly.

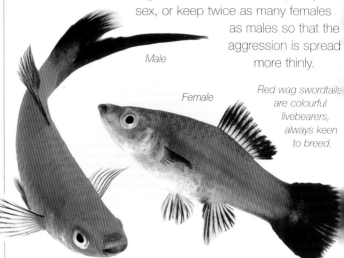

Male

Female

Red wag swordtails are colourful livebearers, always keen to breed.

Reducing the risk of predation

Most fish feed on a wide variety of food types, and this includes other fish! Many bigger fish, especially the larger cichlids, are active predators that hunt down their prey, but virtually all fish will happily eat easy-to-catch species that are small enough to fit in their mouths. When choosing your fish, it is wise to stick to species that all grow to a similar size to avoid predation in the aquarium.

FISH BEHAVIOUR

Above: Cockatoo dwarf cichlids (male shown left) use a 'cave' for breeding and will defend their young against much larger fish.

Staking out territories

Not all fish are territorial; this trait is normally seen in cichlids, some catfish, loaches and gouramis. In the wild, being territorial makes sense; it means securing the best feeding grounds or chasing fish away from a site where young are being guarded. Some fish, such as the dwarf cichlids, only hold small territories and can normally be kept in a community aquarium without harm; others may be heavily territorial and only suited to larger tanks.

Shoaling is a natural instinct

Almost all small, open-water fish, including barbs, tetras, danios and rasboras, are shoaling species, meaning they prefer to be kept in larger groups. in the wild this helps them to avoid predators and find food more quickly (ten pairs of eyes are better than one). In the aquarium you must also keep these fish in groups; on their own, they may become stressed, reclusive and may eventually fall ill. In any case, shoaling fish often look better in groups, becoming more active and displaying brighter colours.

Right: Keep rummy-nose tetras in groups of five or more. In the right water conditions, these peaceful, shoaling fish sport a striking red coloration around the head and distinctive tail stripes. The red area fades when the fish are stressed.

CHOOSING A TANK

Style or substance?

There are many aquarium designs to choose from, some of which cater to the 'lifestyle' market with unusual designs, such as wall-mounted picture frame tanks, circular aquariums and coffee table-style tanks. Without doubt, the most important aspect to consider is the tank's suitability for the fish that will be spending their lives within it. Unfortunately, many of the more unusual aquariums are not designed with this in mind. Consider how easy the aquarium will be to maintain, how much room there is for fish and decor, and whether the tank will be free from vibrations.

Above: A hexagonal tank occupies little floor space, but will accommodate a small shoal of White Cloud Mountain minnows.

Use the spirit level from side to side and back to front.

Above: Levelling the tank is vital. Any unevenness will show when the tank is filled.

Safety and access

If you intend to set up a large aquarium, make sure the floor is strong enough to support its weight and only use cabinets specifically designed for large aquariums. There should be an electrical socket nearby and plenty of room around the aquarium to access all the equipment for maintenance. When you place your tank in its final location, make sure it is level before you fill it. If the aquarium does not have a raised base, be sure to place a layer of polystyrene or plastic foam between the glass base and the cabinet. Remember that once the tank is filled, it is extremely heavy and very difficult to move.

Right: Always stand a glass tank on a layer of polystyrene or foam mat to even out any imperfections in the base board.

Siting the aquarium

Before you buy an aquarium, you must select a suitable location for it, since this will dictate the size and shape of tank you can accommodate. Choose a site away from any sources of heat (which may cause fluctuations in water temperature) and sudden movement, such as doorways, which can stress the fish. Vibrations also upset fish, since they are amplified through water and easily picked up by the fish's lateral line system. For this reason, avoid placing the tank near hi-fi equipment, televisions and domestic appliances. Avoid a site in direct sunlight, since this may cause algae or heat problems during the summer.

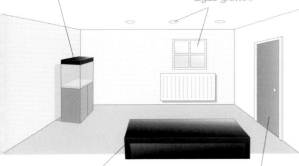

This is the ideal corner location in this room. You will need electrical sockets nearby.

Fitting dimmer switches reduces the shock of sudden lighting changes. Sunlight stimulates algae growth.

Avoid locating the tank near a TV or loudspeakers.

Doors opening and closing suddenly can stress fish.

All-in-one tanks

Many stores offer 'all-in-one' solutions, where the aquarium is supplied complete with all the essential equipment required to prepare it for the fish. These usually represent much better value for money than buying the items separately, and eliminate the worry of making sure you choose the right filters, heaters, lights and other equipment.

WATER AND ELECTRICITY
Be very careful when using water and electricity. A good safety tip is to make sure that any cables are positioned with a 'drip loop', where the cable hangs below the plug socket so that any water running down the cable does not enter the socket.

Above: Fishkeepers today have a wide choice of aquarium shapes and sizes, with or without a purpose-built stand or cabinet.

BIG IS BEST
A large volume of water is much more stable than a small one. Temperature changes occur more slowly and any pollution is diluted. It is often easier, therefore, to keep a larger tank than a smaller one.

CURVES COST
Standard rectangular tanks are easy to manufacture and therefore cheaper to buy, while curved glass or many-sided tanks are more expensive. Rectangular tanks also have a greater viewing area and are usually easier to decorate.

GOLD MEDAL TIPS

18

COVERING UP

A transparent cover-slide placed between the tank and the hood or light unit will help to reduce evaporation, prevent fish from jumping out and protect wooden hoods from warping. Most modern light units are water-proofed and designed to cope with water splashing or condensing on the tubes.

A transparent cover-slide.

LIGHT TIMERS

Fish need a regular day/night cycle, which can be achieved by using an automatic timer. Although they do not sleep like us, they do enter a sleeplike state at night, which is important for their health. Aim to have the light on for 10-12 hours a day and make sure that there is some light in the room when the aquarium light switches on or off to avoid sharp and sudden changes in light levels.

OVERHEATING

In summer, aquariums can easily overheat during hot spells, causing a loss of oxygen and significant problems for your fish. On these days you can switch off the lights and use a small fan near the tank to ensure maximum ventilation.

Filtration is vital

A filter is essential for your tank; without a filtration system of some type, running 24 hours a day, you will be unable to keep fish properly. A basic filter draws water through a sponge, which traps waste particles and keeps the water looking clean. In addition, beneficial bacteria grow on the sponge (or on other filter material in larger filters) and these remove harmful pollutants, making the water safe for your fish. There are several types of filter on the market; internal filter are suitable for small tanks, but external filters provide much better filtration in larger aquariums.

Water outflow

Filter media in layers

Water drawn in

Internal filter
Suitable for the smaller aquarium. The foam insert becomes colonised with bacteria.

Pump motor with inlet and outlet tubes.

External filter
Being larger, external filters can house more filter media.

ESSENTIAL EQUIPMENT

Heating the water

Tropical fish are normally found in water at 23-26°C and must be kept at this temperature in an aquarium. To achieve this, use a combined heater and thermostat (heaterstat). Once set, the heaterstat will switch itself on and off as required to maintain the water temperature. Place the heaterstat at an angle in the tank, where there is sufficient water flow to enable an even distribution of heat. Make sure you place the heaterstat well below the water surface so that the heating element is not exposed to air during water changes.

Above: Attach the heaterstat to the glass, leaving a small gap between the bottom of the heater and the substrate.

Lighting brings the tank to life

There is a choice of lighting for aquariums, but a single fluorescent tube will be enough for basic viewing, whilst two tubes will produce a stronger light. You can also buy tubes that produce light specifically to promote plant growth or to intensify the fishes colour patterns. Many aquariums are supplied with suitable lighting already built in, but if you are installing your own, make sure you only use lights designed for aquariums; household lighting is likely to produce too much heat and may shatter if accidentally splashed.

Some lighting systems incorporate fittings within a waterproof compartment, so there is no need for a cover.

Left: Using a bright white tube (bottom) in combination with a 'warmer' colour tube brings out the fishes' colours and encourages plant growth.

TANK FURNISHING

Right: Lime-free gravel, pea gravel of different sizes, coloured chippings and black quartz are all suitable materials.

Choosing the right substrate

The type of substrate, or gravel, you choose should be based on the needs of the fishes and whether you wish to keep live plants.

Avoid any gravel with sharp edges, as these will damage the sensitive barbels of bottom-dwelling fish. Fish prefer natural-looking gravel; indeed, some species feel uneasy amongst bright or coloured gravels, which also detract from their colours. Plants will do better in a smaller-grain substrate and you can also add nutritional supplements to the substrate to improve growing conditions. If you are very keen on live plants, it is worth doing a little extra research, as getting the substrate right is very important, and difficult to change once the aquarium is full of water.

Keep it natural

Whilst fluorescent ornaments and yellow submarines may appeal to some, especially younger children, your fish may not appreciate them. In nature, fish depend on retreats such as wood, rocks and plants for safety, and many avoid bright areas so that they are not visible to predators. Without a suitable environment in the aquarium, they can become stressed and uneasy, which in extreme cases will result in disease and even death. When decorating your tank, a natural approach will keep your fish happy and healthy.

Above: Wood and rocks enhance the aquarium and help the fish to feel at home.
1 Twisted roots
2 Cork bark
3 Bogwood
4 Rounded boulders
5 Small rounded pebbles
6 Slate
7 Washed coal
8 Lava rock
9 Chippings
10 Granite
11 Westmorland rock

Buy rocks and wood from aquatic dealers

Natural rocks and woods are available from aquatic dealers and this is the only place you should buy them. Many unsuitable rock types contain dangerous metals or substances that alter water chemistry, and some woods can rot and pollute the aquarium. The best kind of wood for tanks is bogwood (long-dead tree roots that have been preserved in boggy conditions). It can release tannins that may stain the water brown, but this is not harmful. Soaking bogwood in several changes of clean water before use can help to reduce staining.

Create both space and retreats

When decorating your tank, try to create as many different areas as possible for your fish. Some species prefer caves as hiding spots, while others like to sit under pieces of bogwood or hover amongst dense areas of plants. There are many artificial, but natural-looking, ornaments on sale, designed specifically to provide hiding places. Certain fish actually prefer to be out in the open, so leave them some swimming space, both in the upper and lower regions of the aquarium.

ALL ABOUT WATER

Keeping the water clean

Fish excrete waste in the aquarium, which results in the production of ammonia and nitrites, both of which are toxic to fish. A filter will remove ammonia and nitrite by creating a suitable home for bacteria to grow and 'feed' on these toxins, but this can take a little time. The bacteria that settle in your filter only grow as the waste levels in your aquarium increase. This is why it is important to ensure waste levels build up at a slow and steady rate, which can be achieved by stocking your tank with fish slowly, and taking care to avoid overfeeding your fish.

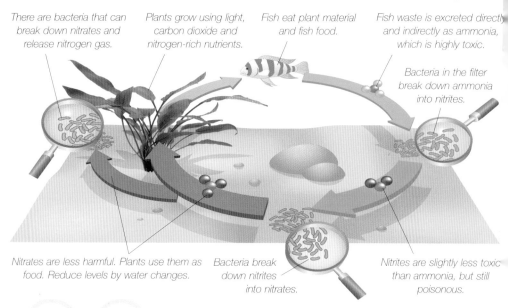

There are bacteria that can break down nitrates and release nitrogen gas.

Plants grow using light, carbon dioxide and nitrogen-rich nutrients.

Fish eat plant material and fish food.

Fish waste is excreted directly and indirectly as ammonia, which is highly toxic.

Bacteria in the filter break down ammonia into nitrites.

Nitrates are less harmful. Plants use them as food. Reduce levels by water changes.

Bacteria break down nitrites into nitrates.

Nitrites are slightly less toxic than ammonia, but still poisonous.

Water testing is an early warning system

The only way to monitor the levels of ammonia and nitrite is to test the tank water regularly. By keeping a close eye on water conditions, you can take action to avoid serious problems before they occur. Modern test kits are relatively quick and easy to use. In a new tank, test for ammonia and nitrite at least twice a week for the first few weeks. Reduce the feeding levels if either of these pollutants are present.

Different kinds of water

Depending on where you live, your tapwater will have varying degrees of minerals present, which makes it either acid, neutral or alkaline, and hard or soft. A fish shop near you will acclimatise the fish you buy to the local water conditions so you can keep them in your aquarium. Some fish, however, can only be kept under certain conditions, and these may be labelled as 'soft water' or 'hard water' species. To keep these more specialised fish, you may need to seek additional advice from your shop.

Above: Rift Valley Lake cichlids need hard water. Before buying any fish, make sure you can provide the right conditions.

Tackling water problems

Most health problems and sudden losses of fish can be traced back to problems with water conditions. If you experience such difficulties, a few steps will help to bring the aquarium back to normal. Small, regular water changes of up to 20% will help dilute toxins in the water, while stopping feeding for a few days will prevent any more waste being produced. Test your water as soon as any problems arise.

Left: Water test kits involve taking a sample of tank water, adding a liquid or tablet reagent and comparing the colour change to the chart provided.

27

28

GOLD MEDAL TIPS

DON'T BE SHY – ASK FOR HELP
If you are unsure about your water conditions or using test kits, most good retailers will allow you to bring in a sample of your aquarium water, which they can test and explain the results for a small charge.

DIRTY FILTERS
If you experience water quality problems with ammonia, nitrites or nitrates, allowing the filter to become a little dirtier than normal can actually help to encourage the useful bacteria to grow.

Tapwater treated for humans needs conditioning for aquarium fish.

NITRATES IN TAPWATER
Some tapwater sources contain high levels of nitrates, which can make it difficult to keep levels low in the aquarium. In these cases water changes are still important, but you may also need to add nitrate-removing filter media to the aquarium. Nitrates are only dangerous for most aquarium fish above 50mg/litre for extended periods.

AQUARIUM PLANTS

Choosing your plants

There are hundreds of
species of aquarium
plant to choose from; some
will only do well under
specialised conditions, while others grow well in all
aquariums, so it is a good idea to ask advice when
you buy them. A few good species to start of with are
vallisneria, hygrophila, anubias, cryptocoryne and Java
mosses and ferns. As a very general rule, plants with
fine, feathered or red leaves are more difficult to keep.

*This dwarf anubias
makes an ideal
foreground plant.*

*Twisted vallisneria
is suitable for the
smaller aquarium.*

*Hygrophilas are
adaptable, fairly
fast-growing plants.*

*Cryptocorynes do
best in stable
water conditions.*

*Above: Remove the lead weight. Gently hold the
plant near the base and, using a finger of the
same hand, make a hole and slide in the plant*

Planting
techniques

Most plants are supplied in
either bunched (loose) or
potted form. Potted plants may cost a little more, but
are often better quality and have established roots. For
potted plants, simply remove the outer pot, leaving the
protective wool around the roots, and place the base of
the plant just beneath the gravel. Bunched plants usually
consist of several individual plants held together by a
weight. Remove the weight, separate out the stems
and plant each one spread out over a larger area.

*Above: There may be up to three pieces
of rockwool, each with two or more plants.*

Creating a display

You can plant your aquarium in any number of styles, and taking a look at other aquariums may help to provide inspiration. A mixture of shapes, sizes and colours can look just as good as large groups of the same plant. A good display usually consists of taller 'background' plants around the back and edges of the tank, smaller 'foreground' plants for the front, floating plants to provide some cover and shade for your fish, and a couple of distinctive 'specimen' plants to provide impact.

Basic plant care

Creating a thriving, fully planted display may take a little extra research, but a few simple tips will help any tank to become a suitable home for hardy plants. The two most important points to consider are the substrate and lighting. The substrate material should be made up of grains between 1 and 2mm in size – roughly between sand and small gravel, while the lighting should consist of a minimum of two fluorescent tubes. You can improve your tank's lighting by replacing the supplied tubes with brighter or special tubes that encourage plant growth and adding a light reflector.

Do plants cause algae?

Since algae often grow on plants, it is easy to assume that plants are the cause of algae problems. In truth plants simply provide a good surface for algae to grow on, since they are in open water, where nutrients are available, and closer to the lights than other surfaces. Once established, plants actually help to combat algae growth by competing for nutrients.

Feeding your plants

Plants in the aquarium get a large proportion of the food they need from the waste produced by your fish, but the regular addition of liquid plant food or fertiliser tablets will help to give your plants an extra boost. Continue using plant fertilisers while your plants are doing well, but cut back if your tank experiences problems with algae.

Above: Place fertiliser tablets under or close to the roots.

Take your time

Since aquarium plants are mainly ornamental, you can start with a few and add more as the tank matures. This way, you can find out which plants do best, and hopefully leave some room to propagate cuttings from successful specimens.

GETTING

Filling the tank

DON'T ADD FOOD TO A NEW AQUARIUM SET-UP
Some people recommend adding small amounts of food to a newly set-up tank to encourage bacteria to grow in the filter, ready for when your fish start producing waste. This is not a good idea, because rotting food will also encourage disease-causing fungus and bacteria to grow.

Once your aquarium and any external equipment are in place you can add the substrate (gravel) before filling the tank. Rinse the substrate first under running tapwater to remove any dust. You can also fill the tank with tapwater, but be sure to use the cold tap to avoid adding metals released by some heating systems. If you use a hosepipe, run the water for a few minutes first to remove any old water from the pipe.

Above: Thoroughly washing gravel substrates is vital to remove dust and debris that will cloud the water.

CLOUDY WATER
It is normal for the water to cloud slightly when you fill your tank and this will usually clear within a day. To reduce clouding you can pour water onto a rock, plate (below) or piece of wood in the tank to avoid disturbing the substrate.

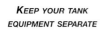

KEEP YOUR TANK EQUIPMENT SEPARATE
You will need buckets, cloths and containers when dealing with aquariums, but never use any items that have been in contact with chemicals of any kind, even if the equipment has been rinsed and dried. To be extra safe, it is best to buy new products and label them for aquarium use only.

Treating the water

Once the tank is partially filled, you can place the heater and filter in position according to the manufacturer' instructions and check everything is working correctly. It is a good idea to add a dechlorinating liquid at this point to remove chlorine, chloramines and heavy metals from the water. (When carrying out water changes, add the dechlorinator to a bucket of water before pouring it into the tank.) Your tank needs time to settle, warm up and stabilise before you add any fish. During this time you can aquascape the tank and plan which fish you intend to keep.

READY FOR FISH

Above: With all the equipment and plants in place, it is tempting to add some fish – but wait at least a week.

How soon can I add my first fish?

When your aquarium has been running for a week it will be ready for its first fish. Now the filter will have to start cleaning up the waste they produce. This process often takes time, since the bacteria need to grow and settle, and the delay can cause dangerous fluctuations in water quality. If you have the patience, you can add a bacterial product to the tank for up to a month before introducing any fish. This 'fishless cycling' allows the filter to mature and greatly reduces problems associated with new aquariums. Only start adding your fish once ammonia and nitrite levels have risen and then dropped to zero.

Left: Using a tapwater conditioner is a quick and reliable method of neutralising the chemicals added to water to make it safe for human consumption.

CHOOSING YOUR FIRST FISH

Make a list

Since there are so many different types of fish to choose from, you will need the advice of a good dealer to help you decide which fish to keep. Take a little time to look at all the fish available and make a list of those you like, even if there are too many for your tank. You can then work out which fish will mix together and which will cause problems, eventually ending up with a suitable selection. That way, you will avoid the disappointment of discovering that a fish you want to add later on is unsuitable for keeping with the stock you already have.

Above: Buy your fish from a reliable aquatic dealer and don't be afraid to ask for advice.

Have a good look at all the fish in the dealer's tank before making a choice.

Choosing healthy fish

Even the best retailers have occasional problems with fish health, so it is important to check the health of the fish before you buy them. Avoid any fish that have cloudy eyes, marks or protrusions on the body, or 'clamped' fins. Most fish should be active and responsive, although some species are naturally quiet, so look to see what the other fish of the same type in the tank are doing. Any individuals that are behaving differently may be ill.

Transporting and introducing fish

Your dealer should package your fish suitably for transport by placing them in plastic bags (ideally with no corners), with more air than water and then into a dark-coloured outer bag. If you are travelling for more than half-an-hour, tell your dealer before your fish are caught so that they can be packaged accordingly. Acclimatising your fish properly is very important and any sudden changes in temperature or light can be very stressful. Turn off your aquarium lights and float the bags in the tank for about 20 minutes before releasing the fish, leaving the lights off for at least another hour.

1 *Examine the fish in the bag to make sure they all look healthy.*

2 *Sealing the bag with a tight knot traps water and air for the journey.*

3 *Travelling in dark surroundings means less stress for the fish.*

Common and scientific names

All aquarium fish have both common and scientific names, but a fish may have several different common names, which can be confusing. When you choose additional fish for your aquarium, you will need to know which fish you already have, so that you can check that any new fish are compatible with your existing stock. It is a good idea to make a note of both the common name and the scientific name of any fish you buy.

GOLD MEDAL TIPS

DO YOUR RESEARCH
Although your dealer should be able to advise you about each species of fish on sale, it is always worth double checking with another source or researching your choices with a good fish species book.

HOW MANY FISH?
Working out a correct fish stocking level for your aquarium can be difficult since there are so many varied factors to consider, and new aquarium technology allows greater stock levels than most popular formulas. The most important factor is to stock slowly, adding only a few fish each week, and follow the advice of your retailer.

Above: Float the unopened bag in the aquarium for 20 minutes before releasing the fish.

ACCLIMATISING THE FISH
Some sources will advise mixing some of your aquarium water with the water in the bag while acclimatising your fish. This is not necessary for freshwater aquariums and may cause undue stress. The only factor that needs equalising is the water temperature; fish will take days or even weeks to adapt to your aquarium conditions.

HOW OFTEN SHOULD I FEED MY FISH?

This depends on their size; small fish require several small feeds a day, whereas large fish require more substantial feeds less often. In the case of a community of small fish, steadily increase the feeding as the tank matures. Start with one feed every other day for the first week and increase this to two or three small feeds a day after a few months.

WHEN TO FEED

Your fish will become used to being fed at set times of day that suit your schedule. Some bottom-dwellers may be semi-nocturnal and feed best in the late evening, while other fish should be fed between one hour after lights on and one hour before lights off.

HOLIDAY FEEDING

In the wild, fish do not always find food every day and adult fish are perfectly capable of surviving happily for a few days without feeding. For longer periods you can use holiday food blocks or automatic feeders (above). If you leave someone else in charge of feeding, make sure they know exactly how much to feed, since non-fishkeepers are likely to overfeed.

A good diet is vital

The phrase 'you are what you eat' applies equally well to fish; a good diet will have a marked effect on their overall health, colour and disease-resistance. Always feed your fish on 'name brand' foods; although they may look the same, cheaper alternatives have a far lower vitamin content, are made from inferior-quality ingredients and will produce more pollutants in the aquarium.

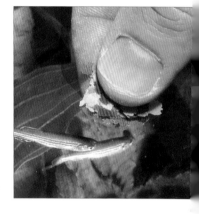

Overfeeding is unkind to fish

The absolute golden rule in fishkeeping is to avoid overfeeding, and this is where most fishkeepers have difficulties. Because almost all the waste produced in an aquarium can be traced back to the food, whether it passes through the fish or not, any overfeeding will cause excess pollution, which results in cloudy water, ill health and a whole host of water quality problems. When you offer your fish food, they should eat it all within one minute. Anything left over or that sinks to the bottom constitutes overfeeding. Always remove uneaten food from the tank.

FEEDING YOUR FISH

A varied diet is more interesting

Above: Daphnia, bloodworms and brineshrimp are good live foods.

Different fish require different types of food, so a varied diet is essential. However, during the first month it is best to stick to simple flake food to avoid any excess waste. After this time, continue to offer flake food as the main part of the diet, since it contains all the essential vitamins and minerals, but supplement the flake with frozen, live, pellet and freeze-dried foods. Sinking wafers and pellets are also available for bottom-dwelling fish, but make sure none is left to decay in the tank.

Freeze-dried mosquito larvae.

Tablet foods. Some 'stick' to the glass.

Flake foods provide a complete diet.

Sinking granules suit bottom-feeding fish.

Freeze-dried tubifex is safe for fish.

Special treats

Many fish relish occasional treats of fresh fruit or vegetables; some algae-eaters, in particular, enjoy grazing on a slice of cucumber. You can buy clips, often called 'lettuce grips', to hold items of food. Place these in a part of the tank where you can see them and remove them easily if the food is not eaten. Only ever feed fresh food items and not manufactured foods and remember that these are only supplements to a proper diet made up of specially prepared dried foods.

Above: Some fish enjoy fresh peas with skins removed, cucumber, courgette and blanched lettuce secured in a clip (left).

REGULAR MAINTENANCE

Why do water changes?

There are two main reasons for carrying out regular water changes in the aquarium: one is to reduce the build-up of nitrates – the end result of filtration – and the other is to replace lost minerals and nutrients that help to stabilise water conditions. The volume and frequency of water changes depends largely on the level of nitrates in the water, so regular water testing is essential. As a basic guide, aim to replace 10-20% of the water every two weeks. Take new water from the cold tap, treat it with a dechlorinator and leave it to warm up to room temperature before using it.

Cleaning the substrate

A large proportion of aquarium waste will settle in the substrate. Live plants in the aquarium use this waste as a source of food, but in open areas it can build up to dangerous levels, encouraging algae and a deterioration in water quality. Using a gravel cleaning device you can disturb and siphon waste from the substrate. Discard the water removed by the siphon or, even better, use it in the garden or on houseplants and count it as a water change. Always remember to turn off the electricity supply before carrying out any work in your aquarium.

Left: As you guide the cleaner over the substrate, the gravel is sucked up into the tube and whirled around in the water flow to separate it from any debris. The heavier particles sink back down to the floor and the more buoyant silt is sucked into the bucket.

Keeping filters clean

Your filter will need regular maintenance to remove trapped waste matter and to keep it in good working order. Clean internal filters every two weeks and external filters once a month. Always rinse sponges and other media in water taken from the aquarium, since the chlorine in tapwater will damage useful filter bacteria. If your filter contains carbon, replace this every few months. The main sponges or biological media will only need replacing once a year. To ensure that bacterial populations remain suitably high, never change more than half the filter's sponges or biological media at any one time.

Above: Rinse the filter sponge in aquarium water, squeezing it until it is clean. Replace it when it no longer keeps its shape.

Establishing a routine

Maintaining a typical community aquarium is relatively easy providing it is done regularly. Creating a weekly routine will help to achieve this aim and reduce the overall time you spend on the aquarium. A basic routine would consist of cleaning algae from the glass *(right)*, gravel cleaning, rinsing filter sponges (in the waste water from gravel cleaning) and topping up with water prepared the day before.

LITTLE AND OFTEN
Aquarium maintenance is essential, both for the fishes' longterm health and the appearance of the aquarium, but should always be done in small steps. An aquarium is a balanced environment that needs time to mature and establish, so avoid any major upheavals as much as possible.

RAINWATER
Never use collected rainwater in the aquarium. Although it is often purer than tapwater, it contains none of the essential minerals needed to maintain stable water conditions. Also, it can contain pollutants picked up from the atmosphere after dry spells, and may even have passed through dead animals in the house guttering.

WHO SHOULD I BELIEVE?
Aquarists are often given conflicting advice on the subjects of water changes and filter maintenance. This is because the correct maintenance for your tank may be different to that of another tank of the same style and size. Regular water testing and the advice of a good dealer will help you achieve the right level of maintenance.

KEEPING FISH HEALTHY

Check your fish for signs of ill-health

Under normal conditions, the fishes' immune systems prevent disease taking hold, but problems occur when a fish becomes stressed, is physically injured or when the background levels of harmful disease organisms rise dangerously. Taking care not to overstock the tank, quarantining new fish, monitoring water conditions and good aquarium maintenance will prevent the outbreak of most diseases.

Slime patches
These are a fish's immune response to skin parasites. Fish may show flicking behaviour and swim with clamped, folded fins. Use an antiparasite treatment.

Fine gold spots
The spots are typical symptoms of velvet disease, caused by a skin parasite. Treat quickly with a targeted antiparasite remedy.

Ragged fin edges
Ragged fins, which may also be red and sore, are signs of a bacterial infection called finrot. Use an antibacterial treatment.

Mouth rot
Cottonwool-like growths round the mouth could be a bacterial or fungal infection. Use a treatment that tackles both.

Fungus
Skin damage may become infected with fungus to produce cottonwool-like growths. Treat for both external bacteria and fungus.

Swollen eyes
These may be caused by an internal bacterial infection and can be seen in fish affected with dropsy. A tumour behind the eye may also cause this symptom.

Rapid gill movement
These could be caused by high nitrite levels or other water quality problems, as well as parasites or bacterial infection. Make a water change if necessary, or treat as appropriate.

White spot
Sugar grain-sized spots on the skin and gills are signs of white spot, a fast-spreading parasite infection. Complete the treatment as directed.

Protruding scales
Swelling with scales protruding like a pinecone, known as dropsy, is caused by an internal bacterial infection that inhibits the fish's ability to control the level of water in its body. Use an internal bacterial treatment.

Avoid stress and poor water conditions

Stress is the biggest cause of disease in the aquarium and can result from a number of factors, including transportation, sudden changes in water conditions, inappropriate decor, aggression from other fish and fluctuations in heating levels. Poor water quality can trigger health problems because the fish's immune system overreacts to pollutants in the water and continually fights a losing battle. Always remedy the cause of any disease before treating the symptoms, because as long as stress or poor water quality factors are present, treatments are often ineffective.

Making the most of treatments

Before using a treatment, carry out basic maintenance and remove any carbon or chemical media from the filter, since these will also absorb treatments. Some treatments can decrease the amount of available oxygen in the aquarium, so keep the water surface moving as much as possible to increase aeration. Always carry out the whole course of any treatment you use according to the manufacturer's instructions. Some diseases have a 'life cycle' and a full course of treatment is designed to prevent reinfection. After using a course of treatment, carry out a small water change and replace any carbon or chemical media. Avoid using two treatments at the same time, as the combined effect of many common treatments can be dangerous, although you can continue to use dechlorinators or plant fertilisers.

Left: Dilute the correct amount of medication in aquarium water before adding it to the tank to avoid localised high concentrations.

HOSPITAL TANKS
A common method of treating fish is to set up a separate 'hospital tank', where affected fish can live in isolation while they are treated. This will only work if the tank is set up with water from the main aquarium and with a matured filter. Adding hiding spots will also aid recovery.

Above: A hospital tank with an air-powered, twin-sponge filter can double as a quarantine tank.

SUDDEN DEATHS
Diseases usually take time to affect fishes; look out for signs such as loss of appetite accompanied by obvious physical symptoms. However, sudden deaths are usually the result of pollutants in the water that may not be easy to test for. You can buy special 'polishing' media for filters to remove unusual pollutants.

RESTOCKING
It is a good idea to wait at least a few weeks after any outbreak of disease before restocking. New fish are heavily weakened by the process of transport and acclimatisation and are more likely to be affected by anything left in the water that could cause disease.

Further Information

Recommended Books

Alderton, David, *Starter Aquarium* (Interpet Publishing, 2002)

Dawes, John, *Complete Encyclopedia of the Freshwater Aquarium* (Interpet Publishing, 2001)

Expert team, *500 Ways to be a Tropical Fishkeeper* (Interpet Publishing, 2005)

Sandford, Gina, *Tankmaster Guide to Setting up Your Tropical Freshwater Aquarium* (Interpet Publishing, reprinted 2003)

Sandford, Gina, *Mini Encyclopedia of the Tropical Freshwater Aquarium* (Interpet Publishing, 2004)

Sandford, Gina, *Q & A Manual of the Tropical Freshwater Aquarium* (Interpet Publishing, 2000)

Thraves, Stuart, *Setting up a Tropical Aquarium* (Interpet Publishing, 2004)

Setting up an Aquarium – A Complete Pet Owner's Manual (Barron's, 2000)

Clubs

Federation of British Aquatic Societies (FBAS), 44 Weeks Road, Ryde,
    Isle of Wight PO33 2TL

Federation of American Aquarium Societies (FAAS), 4816 East 64th Street,
    Indianapolis, IN 46220-4728

Recommended Websites

http://www.fbas.co.uk
http://www.fishlinkcentral.com
http://www.fishtanksandponds.net
http://www.ornamentalfish.org
http://www.thinkfish.co.uk

Picture Credits